Juilliard Rehabilitating 'Antony and Cleopatra'

NY Times————————2/2/75

By DONAL HENAHAN

Ever since Sept. 16, 1966, when the Metropolitan Opera christened its new house at Lincoln Center with a hair-curlingly awful production of Samuel Barber's "Antony and Cleopatra," the suspicion has been growing that the work itself might not be as bad as it seemed on that premiere night. Could anything be that bad, really? The night has gone down in the annals of opera as a landmark of vulgarity and staging excesses.

Mr. Barber's score, as we discovered from subsequent exposure to revised excerpts in concert and on records, was to a great extent an innocent victim of the over-all fiasco. And Thursday night at the Juilliard Theater, the composer's extensively rewritten work went a long way toward escaping entirely from the shadow of its dismal premiere. Under the energizing conducting of James Conlon, the Juilliard American Opera Center did a magnificent job of rehabilitation.

Since "Antony and Cleopatra" was so generally despised at birth, the tendency now may be to overvalue it. That would be no service to anyone. But as presented in this drastically cut and reworked version, the opera held interest throughout. In more leisurely days, almost all operas were rewritten several times, and that includes many of the staples of the repertory. Mr. Barber's work might still benefit from a bit of tinkering, even though as it stands it provides a respectable evening of musical theater, with flashes of eloquence and power.

The original, you may remember, had a libretto by Franco Zeffirelli, who also devised the sets and costumes and directed the Cecil B. De-Mille production with its moving pyramids, camels, horses, clowns and goats. (If you do not remember that night, you are no true circus lover.)

The revised work has discreetly dropped Mr. Zeffirelli, and even his libretto has been, as the composer puts it, "completely transformed" by Gian Carlo Menotti, who also directed the new production. The sets now, rather than being a series of stunningly inappropriate imitatios of abstract sculpture, are relatively simple, if nowhere strikingly original or even consistently evocative of Cleopatra's Egypt.

However, the sets do suggest a grimly bloody mood, since the designer, Pasquale Grossi, uses throughout a brownish red or tortoise shell for the drops, Cleopatra's throne, her monument and just about every other surface that needs covering. Marble, in both tortoise shell and white, dominates nearly every scene. The costumes, similarly, are unremarkable but elaborate enough to pass grand opera muster. Nothing remotely suggests the gargantuan ugliness of the costume in which the Zeffirelli production encased Leontyne Price, the Cleopatra (a gown that, as one recalls it, made her look like an incipient mummy).

In revising the score, Mr. Barber says, he tried to tighten the two basic elements of the opera, the political and the amorous, "combining them into one and, in general, giving more space to the lovers. In other words, more Egypt than Rome."

Since the premiere he has also added some music even though he cut at least an hour from the original. Ten characters, all minor, have been eliminated, so that the work now moves with a greater sense of purpose and more clarity. In one notable change, Cleopatra no longer dies melodramatically in midphrase, but is given a short but poignant coda full of sensuous longing and possibly remorse.

The Juilliard cast, led by Roland Hedlund and Esther Hinds in the title parts, might have been improved upon here and there. Enoch Sherman's Caesar was anything but an imperial, domineering figure onstage and the voice sounded strained at times. The English of the chorus could rarely be grasped, chiefly owing to Mr. Barber's way of clotting his concerted numbers with many-layered texts and contorted rhythms.

But over-all the score's vocal and theatrical difficulties were overcome with surprising success. Miss Hinds, a suitably lithe and seductive Cleopatra, has a lovely lyric soprano that she often used to good effect; it was a bit light, however, for the light heavyweight demands placed on it in several dramatic scenes. Mr. Hedlund, a convincingly passion-crazed Roman, was equally adept in the love scenes and in full battle cry.

The opera, in its reconstruction, forms a pyramid: a weak first act, a generally strong second act, and a third that (in this performance, at least) trails off into some pretty thin music until it is redeemed by Cleopatra's "What should I stay . . . in this vile world." Three additional performances, all sold-out, are scheduled: tonight, tomorrow (matinee) and Monday night.

SAMUEL BARBER

ANTONY AND CLEOPATRA

(REVISED EDITION)

SCHIRMER

REVISED EDITION

ANTONY AND CLEOPATRA

Opera in Three Acts

Music by
SAMUEL BARBER

Text of
William Shakespeare

VOCAL SCORE

Piano Reduction by the Composer

G. SCHIRMER
New York · London

NOTE

ANTONY AND CLEOPATRA was commissioned by the Metropolitan Opera Association for the opening of the new Metropolitan Opera House in Lincoln Center, New York, on September 16, 1966.

G. SCHIRMER, INC.

866 Third Avenue

New York, N.Y. 10022

CAST OF CHARACTERS

CLEOPATRA, Queen of Egypt . . . . *Soprano*

OCTAVIA, Caesar's sister . . . . *Non-singing*

CHARMIAN, Cleopatra's attendant . . . . *Mezzo-Soprano*

IRAS, Cleopatra's attendant . . . . *Contralto*

ANTONY, a Roman general · · · . . . . *Baritone*

CAESAR (Octavius), ruler of Rome . . . . *Tenor*

AGRIPPA, a senator . . . . *Bass*

ENOBARBUS, his friend . . . . *Bass*

EROS, Antony's shield-bearer . . . *a young man's voice (Tenor or High Baritone)*

DOLABELLA, an officer of Antony . . . . *Baritone*

THIDIAS, Caesar's ambassador . . . . *Tenor or High Baritone*

A SOLDIER of CAESAR . . . . *Baritone or Bass*

A RUSTIC . . . . *Baritone or Bass*

A MESSENGER . . . . *Tenor*

A SOOTHSAYER . . . . *Bass*

ALEXAS, Cleopatra's attendant . . . . *Bass*

FIRST GUARD . . . . *Baritone*

SECOND GUARD . . . . *Tenor*

THIRD GUARD . . . . *Bass*

FOURTH GUARD . . . . *Bass*

FIRST WATCHMAN . . . . *Bass*

SECOND WATCHMAN . . . . *Bass*

DANCERS

SYNOPSIS OF SCENES

Act I

Act II

Act III

to Orazio Orlando

Antony and Cleopatra

William Shakespeare

Prologue

Samuel Barber
Op. 40
Revised Edition

The stage is in darkness. The chorus is grouped
on either side of the stage and sings from there
throughout the opera (except at the end of Act I,
when it is required to sing offstage).

*Throughout this score a ⌐——¬ in the vocal part (although without a *3*) signifies a triplet.

46074c

4

wastes The night in rev - el; _____

wastes The night in rev - el; _____

wastes The night in rev - el; _____

wastes The night in rev - el; _____

SOPRANO
An - to - ny fish - es, An - to - ny drinks, — and

ALTO
An - to - ny fish - es, An - to - ny drinks, — and

An - to - ny fish - es, An - to - ny drinks, and

TENOR div.
An - to - ny fish - es, An - to - ny drinks, and

BASS div.
An - to - ny fish - es, An - to - ny drinks, and

An - to - ny fish - es, An - to - ny drinks, and

8

12

46074

To Rome,___ to Rome,___ to Rome.___

To Rome,___ to Rome,___ to Rome.___

div.
To Rome,___ to Rome,___ to Rome.___

div.
To Rome,___ to Rome,___ to Rome.___

(As the light on the stage slowly increases, Antony is shown surrounded by pretty female attendants and slaves who are busy combing and perfuming his hair and painting his nails. Nearby, sprawled on the steps leading to a throne, Enobarbus is half asleep in the arms of a young Nubian girl.)

Scene 1

(A room in Cleopatra's Palace.)

Antony, Enobarbus.

Con moto ♩ = 100

(Pushing aside his attendants, Antony gets up and throws to the ground the garland that has just been placed on his head.)

Antony **Recit** *(free)* *f (rather fast, impetuously)*

These strong E-gyp-tian fet-ters__ I must

a tempo

break Or__ lose my-self in dot-age.__ I must__

(Slaves and attendants scatter in fright and disappear into the inner palace.)

__ from this en-chant-ing queen__ break off; I must with haste from

(Enobarbus lazily frees himself from the Nubian girl, who is reluctant to part from him.)

hence.

Enobarbus *f (roughly)*

Why, then we kill our wom-en.__ If they suf-fer our de-

An.

I must be gone.

Eno.

par-ture,___ death's the word.___

Cle-o-pa-tra,

8
Flowing

mf espr.

Eno.

catch-ing but the least noise___ of this, dies in-stant-ly: I have seen her die

simile

Eno.

twen-ty times ___ up-on far poor-er mo-ment. I do

Eno.

think there is met-tle in death,___ she has such a ce-ler-i-ty in

(Once more Antony throws the garland away, pushing Enobarbus aside.)

Antony: Would I_____ had nev - er___ / Would I had nev - er seen___ of__ pure__ love.

An.: seen her!_____ / her!_____

Eno.: Salt Cle - o - pa - tra!

An. I shall break The cause of our ex-pe-dience___ To the Queen,

An. and get her leave to part. I must be gone!___

(As they start off they are stopped short by the appearance of Cleopatra, who slowly advances from the inner courts of the palace followed by Charmian, Iras and the rest of her court. Exit Enobarbus.)

9

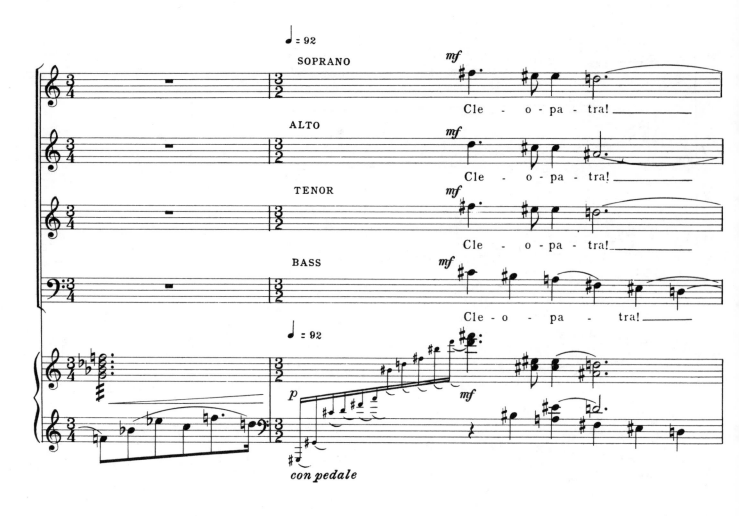

(Cleopatra slowly enters the room, ignoring Antony's presence.)

(Suddenly confronted by him, she stops and swoons, as if about to fall. She is quickly supported by Charmian and Iras, who then lead her to the throne. Antony meekly follows her, and sinks at her feet.)

24

46074

(*Freeing herself from Antony's embrace, Cleopatra slowly gets up and descends from the throne, followed by Antony.*)

28

46074

30

(After one last embrace, Antony quickly leaves. Cleopatra follows him to the door and leaning against it watches him disappear.

Very slow blackout.)

46074

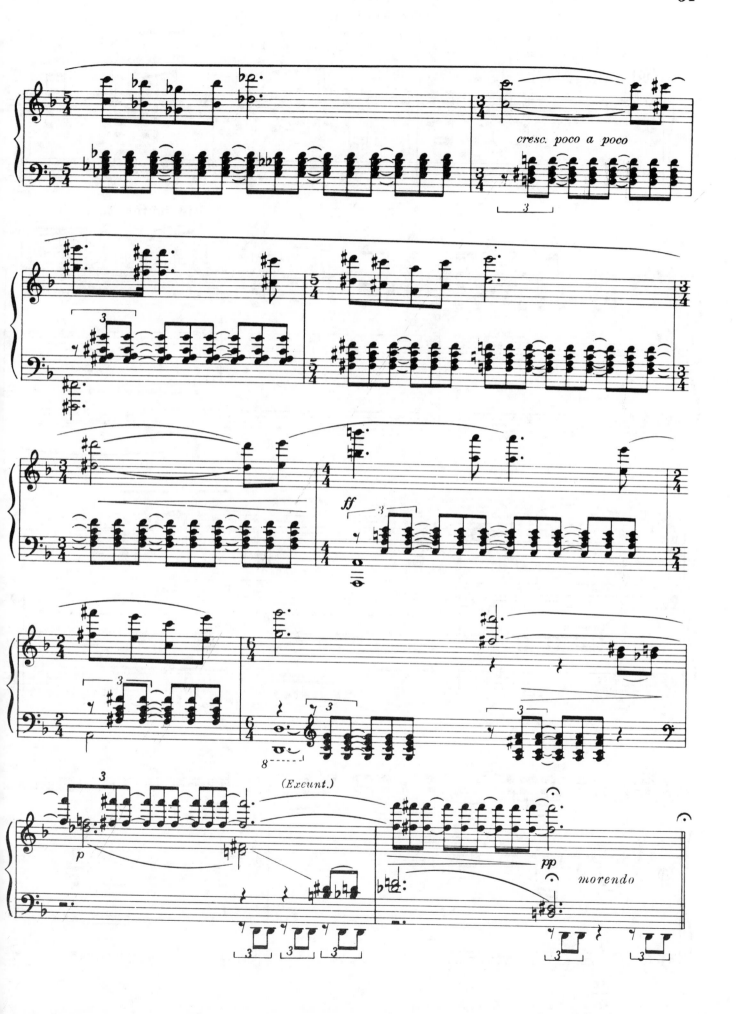

cresc. poco a poco

ff

(Exeunt.)

p

pp

morendo

Scene 2
The Senate in Rome

(Groups of Senators, obviously tense and excited, stand in the middle of the Senate.
Caesar enters, greeted by all, and joins one of the groups.)

(Caesar's entrance is followed almost immediately by that of Antony, who is accompanied by Enobarbus. As they advance onto the Senate floor they are greeted and embraced warmly by some old friends. As Antony comes face to face with Caesar there is a moment of embarrassment, but Antony's disarming smile breaks Caesar's initial hostility and the two embrace each other.)

TENOR: Ah!

Chorus

BASS: Ah!

Hail, —— Mar-cus An - ton - i - us!

Hail, —— Mar-cus An - ton - i - us!

36

*(Maecenas steps down from his seat,
and goes to Caesar, trying to calm him.)*

Cae. You have_brok-en The ar-ti-cle of your_oath, which you shall nev-er Have tongue to charge me with.

An. _strife.

(Antony waves Maecenas away.)

An. No, Mae-ce-nas; let Cae-sar speak now. The ar-ti-cle_ of my

20

Cae. To lend_me arms and aid when I re-quired them, The which you both de-nied._

An. oath...? Neg-lect-ed rath-er; and

(Worried by the quarrel, which has become increasingly threatening, some of the Senators approach Caesar and Antony, trying to separate them.)

Cae. No more__ than my re-sid-ing here at Rome _____ Might be to you in

An. __ to you? __

TENOR

Soft, Cae-sar!

Soft, Cae - sar!

BASS

poco f

Soft, Cae - sar!

Soft,

poco f

sfp

21

Cae. E-gypt. Yet if__ you there did plot a-gainst my

An. As near-ly as I may, I'll play the pen-i-tent to you. But mine hon

BASS

Cae-sar! __

21

f

42

46074

(All the Senators, except Agrippa, return to their seats.)

24

(The Senators show great surprise.
Enobarbus approaches Antony to counsel him.)

Agr. un-slip- ping knot, take An - to-ny Oc - ta -

Agr. - via to his wife; whose beau-ty

Agr. — claims No worse a hus-band than the best of men;

Cae. - tra heard you...

Antony *(in a conciliatory manner)* *f* (with con-

I am not mar-ried,__ Cae-sar:__ let me

10

26

trolled impatience) *(Agrippa gestures Caesar and*

An. hear A-grip-pa____ fur - ther speak.____

Antony to him and with his arms on their shoulders walks away
with them, followed by the rest of the Senators, murmuring aloud.)

Scene 3

Another room in Cleopatra's Palace

(Cleopatra, surrounded by her court, including Charmian and Iras. Games are being played by some of the attendants, while other slaves are busy with household chores such as weaving, etc.)

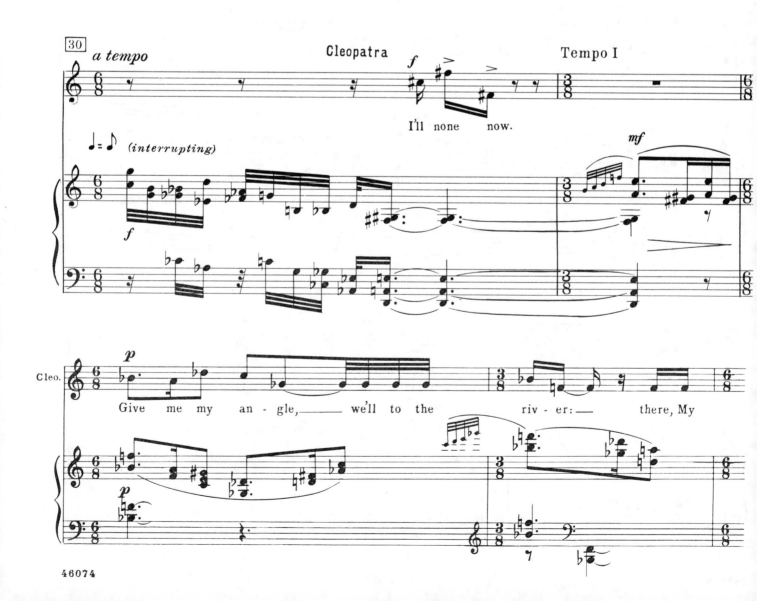

mu-sic play-ing far off,_____ I will be-tray Taw-ny-finned fish-

es.____ And as I draw them up,____

___ I'll think them ev'-ry one___ an An-to-ny, And say,___ "Ah, ha!

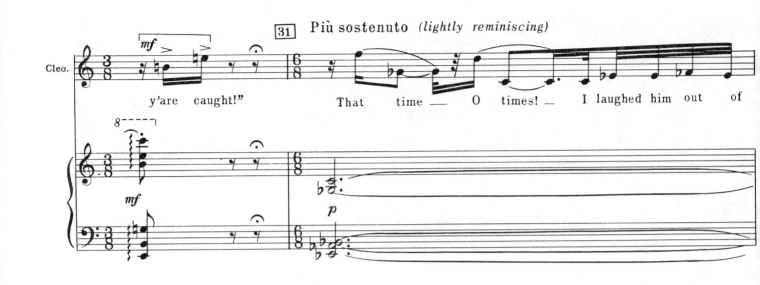

y'are caught!" That time — O times! — I laughed him out of

pa-tience; and that night — I laughed him in-to pa-tience.

(caressing)

And the next morn ere the ninth hour — I drunk him — to his bed: —

(Charmian hands Cleopatra a golden cup of spiced wine.)

— Then put my crown and man-tles on him, — While I wore his sword Phil - ip - pan. —

(suddenly serious)

My man of men!

Char-mi - an! —

32 Tempo I

Tempo I

(After

drinking from the cup Cleopatra hands it back to Charmian.)

(sensuously)

Give me to drink man-drag - o - ra. —

46074

so— he— calls ———— me.)

mp espr.

36 *(with increasing ardor and expansion)*

p

Now ———— I feed my-self —— with most de-li-cious

poi - son.

(with pathos)

Think on me, —— That am with Phoe-bus'— am'rous pinch-es

black, And wrin - kled deep in

58

(She slowly returns to her couch.)

37 Tempo I, flowing

Cleo. Give — me some mu - sic,

Cleo. mu - sic, mood-y food _____ Of us ___ that trade in

poco allarg.

a tempo

Cleo. love. _____

morendo

46074

(As the slaves resume their dance a Messenger, ushered in by two guards, timorously approaches Cleopatra

Tempo del Ballo (♩ = 100)

attacca subito

simile

and hands her a tablet.)

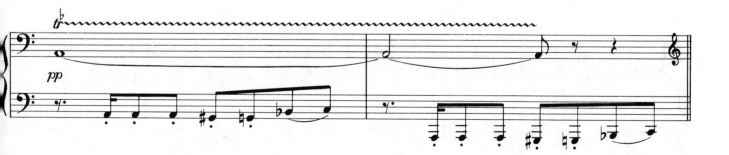

46074

60

(Having read the message, Cleopatra, with a cry of rage, flings the tablet onto the floor. Then, having rushed to the palace eunuch, snatches the whip from him and mercilessly flays the Messenger. The terrified court scatters in cowering groups.)

46074

Cleopatra *(free, fast)*

The most in-fec-tious pes- ti-lence up-on you!

Messenger *(crawling*

Good mad-am, pa-tience.

colla voce

away from the lashes of her whip)

a tempo 40 *(strikes him)*

What say you?

Cleo. Hence, _____ hor - ri - ble vil - lain, hence, — or I'll kick thine

Cleo. eyes: I will un - hair thy head. Thou shalt be

Ossia:

brine, Smart - ing in pick - le.

Cleo. whipped with wire, _____ and stewed in brine, Smart-ing in ling'-ring pick-le.

Messenger

Grac - ious

Cleopatra (softly)

Is he mar-ried?

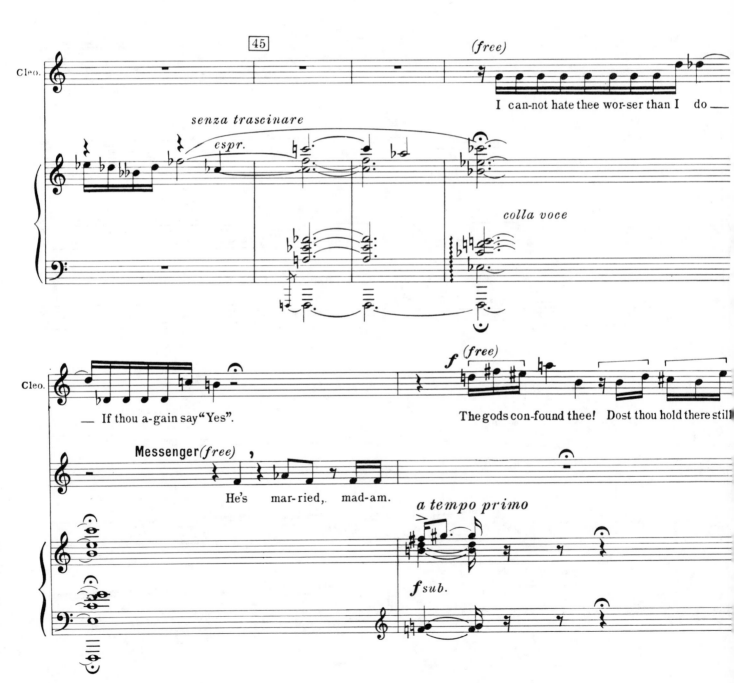

I can-not hate thee wor-ser than I do —

— If thou a-gain say "Yes".

The gods con-found thee! Dost thou hold there still

He's mar-ried, mad-am.

(Everyone shows great surprise.)

(Reassured, and emboldened by curiosity, most of the attendants reapproach Cleopatra.)

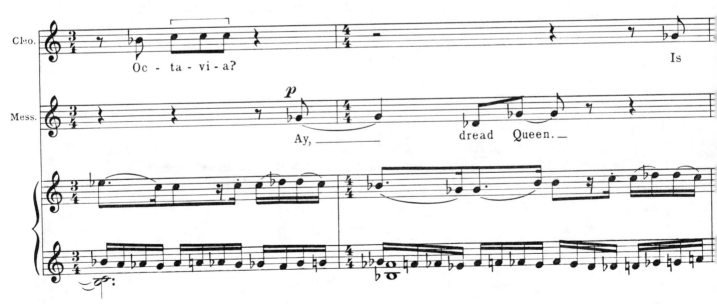

she as tall as me?

She is not, mad-am.

Iras

She is

Didst hear her speak?

not.

She is not.

Charmian

She is not.

a tempo

espr., un poco sost.

Cleo. I faint.— Pit-y me, Char-mian,

allarg. poco a poco fino alla fine

Cleo. but do not speak to me. Lead — me to my cham -

(Supported by Charmian and Iras, she exits, followed by the entire court.)

52 **Allegro con pathos irrequieto** ♩=126

Cleo. ber.——

46074

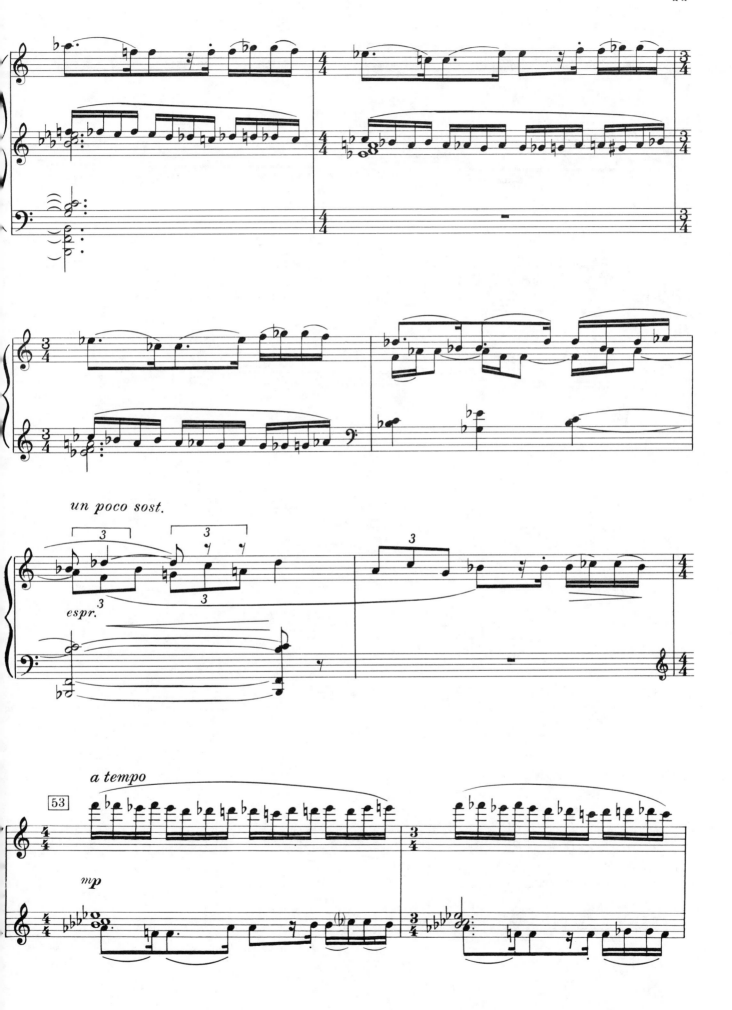

Scene 4
A Roman Banquet Hall. Night.

(At one table, Antony, Caesar, Octavia and a few Patricians with their wives. At another table, soldiers and younger Senators, among them Eros and Enobarbus. In the light of guttering torches the very noisy banquet is obviously at an end. Among the soldiers are overt signs of drunkenness.)

(As Caesar rises to speak the soldiers stand at attention and the noise suddenly dies down.)

*(Followed by the other women and the old
Patrician couples, Octavia rises to leave.
Antony accompanies her to the door.)*

on. Be cheer - ful. My Oc-ta vi- a,

Read not my blem-ish-es in the world's re-port: I have not kept my

square, but that to come Shall be done by the

(Octavia, having returned his greeting, departs, accompanied by Caesar and the other guests who have followed her.

An.

rule.   Good night, dear la -dy.

Antony then returns to the room and joins the remaining soldiers and Senators, some of whom are now sprawled on the floor totally drunk.)

Enobarbus (aside, ironically)

Hap - pi-ly,___   a-

Dolabella (taking Enobarbus aside)
(free, dreaming)

Now he must leave Cle-o-pa-tra ut-ter-ly.

Eno.

men.   Nev - er;   he will not.

decisivo

free

colla voce

46074

(Eros, who has begun to detect signs of anxiety on Antony's face, pours wine into his cup, trying to comfort him.)

He will to his E-gypt--ian dish a-gain.

Age can-not with-er her, ___ nor cus-tom stale Her in-fi-nite va-ri-e-ty.

Dolabella
She's a most tri-um-phant la-dy, if __ re-port square to her.

(*Pushing Eros aside, Antony leaves his drinking companions and comes forward to sit alone in a corner of the room, his face darkened by anguish. Enobarbus and Dolabella, joined by the half-drunk Thidias, move farther away, so as not to be overheard.*)

100

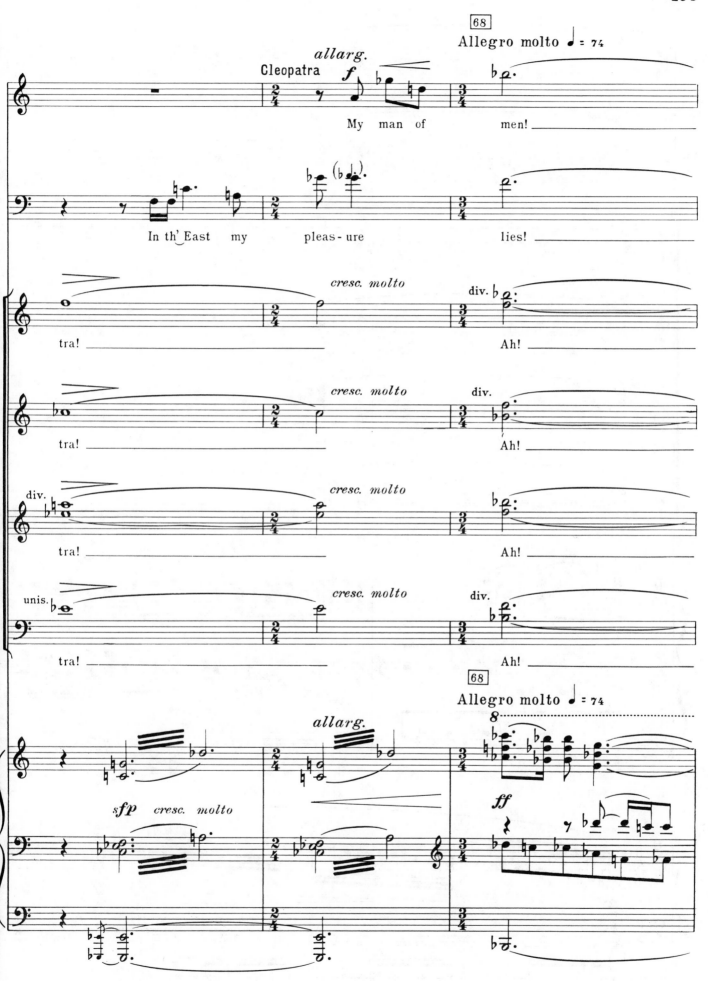

Act Two

Scene 1

Rome. The Senate.

(Caesar holds the floor, surrounded by excited groups of Senators.)

She in the ha-bil'-ments of the god-dess I - sis That day ap-peared.

con pedale

Un - to her he gave the stab-lish-ment of E - gypt; made her of low-er Syr - ia,

Ah!

Of E-gypt!

Ah!

Of E-gypt!

(A messenger runs in and hands Caesar a tablet. Caesar reads and contemptuously hands it to the nearest group of Senators. They pass it from one to another in disbelief.)

king, A - dal - las: King Man-chus of A - ra - bi - a;

king, A - dal - las: King Man-chus of A - ra - bi - a;

(Another messenger runs in and gives Caesar another tablet.)

intensificando sempre

TENOR I

ff

Her - od of Jew-ry; Mith-ri - da-tes, king of Com-a-gene; the kings

TENOR II

ff

Her - od of Jew-ry; King of Pont; king of Com-a-gene; the kings

BASS *ff*

Her - od of Jew - ry; King of Pont; Po - le - mon and A - myn - tas, the

intensificando sempre

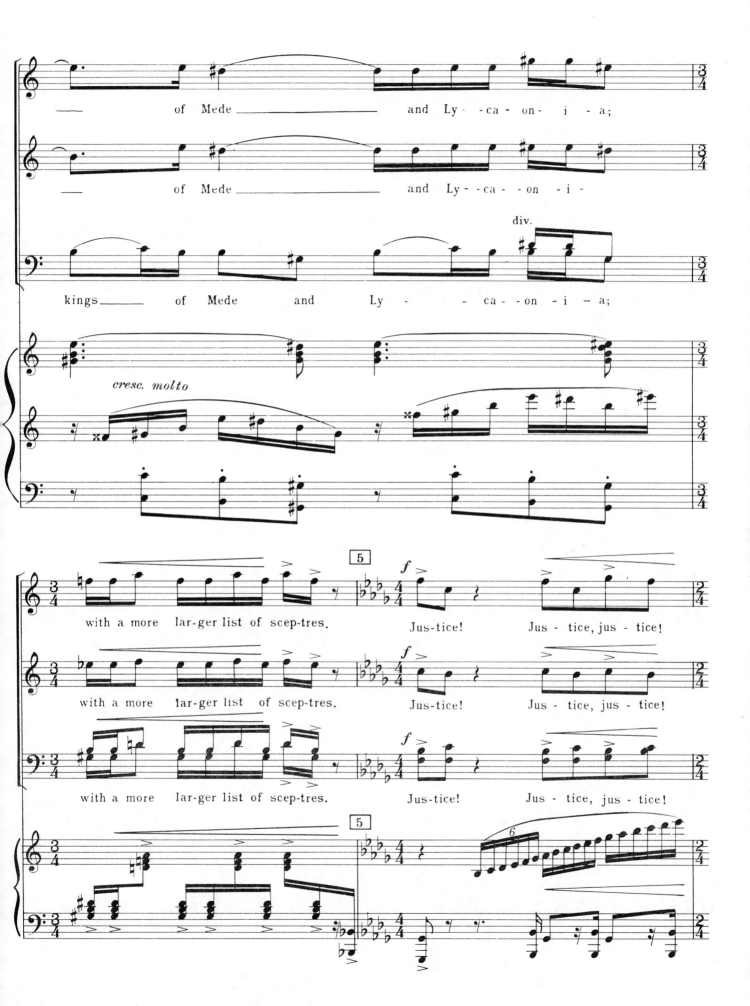

114

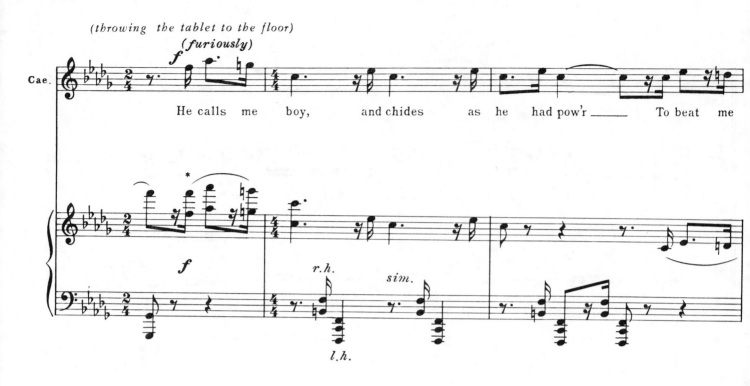

(throwing the tablet to the floor)
(furiously)

Cae. He calls me boy, and chides as he had pow'r _____ To beat me

Cae. out of E - gypt. Let our best heads

TENOR
Jus-tice!

BASS
Jus-tice!

*Throughout this section the ♪ should be very short.

Scene 2

Alexandria

Charmian, Iras, other attendants, slave girls and the chief eunuch by a pool in Cleopatra's palace garden.

(They drag the Soothsayer to the edge of the pool and force him to sit down. He is immediately surrounded by all the girls who vie with each other to have their palms read.)

He means in

You shall be yet far fair - er than you are.

flesh.

Wrin-kles for-bid!

Iras

No,— you shall paint when you are old.—

Alexas

Vex not his pre - science,— be at -

122

46074

124

46074

(As the Soothsayer

mf (mocking)
A-men, dear god-dess, hear that pray-er of the peo-ple! A-men.

walks off everyone breaks into wild laughter.)

Vivace

Iras
Hush, here come the Queen and An-to-ny!

(Enter Antony and Cleopatra holding each other tenderly. The girls and the eunuch run away giggling.)

Moderato ♩=66

mp sensuously

p espr.

I'll set a bourn how far___ to be be-lov-ed.___
reck-oned.___ Then
must thou needs find out new heav-en, new
earth.
tell me how much...___
There's

mf *poco f* *poco f* *mf* *molto espr.*

3074

(to Enobarbus)

An. To-mor-row, sol-dier,— By sea and land I'll fight:

An. or I will live,_____ Or bathe my dy - ing hon-or_ in the

16 Allegro molto, alla marcia ♩=120

(Exit Antony.)

An. blood That shall make it live a - gain._____

(As Enobarbus tries to follow Antony Cleopatra stops him.)

Cleopatra (to Enobarbus)

I will be e - ven with thee, doubt it not._

Thou hast op-posed my be-ing in these

Enobarbus But why, why, why?

wars, And say'st it is not fit. Is't not de-nounced a-

Well, is it, is it?

gainst us? Why should not we Be

134

46074

ff *appassionato*

138

46074

Scene 3

Outside Antony's battlefield tent

Guards (3 Soli)

Guard I

The night Is shin-y, and they

♩=84

sempre staccato

I

say we shall em-bat-tle Cae-sar ___ By the sec-ond hour.

Guard III

This

It will de-ter-mine one way.

Guard II *(sotto voce)*

It will de-ter-mine one way.

(sotto voce)

day will prove A shrewed one to us: fare you well.

Noth-ing. What

Heard you of noth-ing strange— a-bout the camp?

sempre stacc.

Walk; ___ let's see if oth-er watch-men _ Do hear what we do.

Walk; ___ let's see if oth-er watch-men _ Do hear what we do.

leaves him.   what we ___

28

How now, mas-ters?

How now, mas-ters?

___ do.   How   now, mas-ters?

1st half   How now?   Do you

Chorus (BASS)

2nd half   How now?   Do you

28

Scene 4

Inside the tent

(As the dawn slowly colors the sky the tent opens, revealing Antony and
Cleopatra lying together on a couch in a passionate embrace. At the entrance of the tent
Eros stands guard.)

*)= linger slightly

(lingering)

lentamente
arpeggiato

Cleopatra *mp* * | 31 | Tranquillo ♩ = 72

Oh take, oh — take those — lips a -

Antony *mp*

Oh

| 31 | Tranquillo ♩ = 72

p

Cleo.

way ———— That so sweet - ly ———— were — for -

An.

take, oh — take those — lips a - way ———— That so sweet - ly were for-

* *The following two stanzas are by Beaumont and Fletcher.*

152

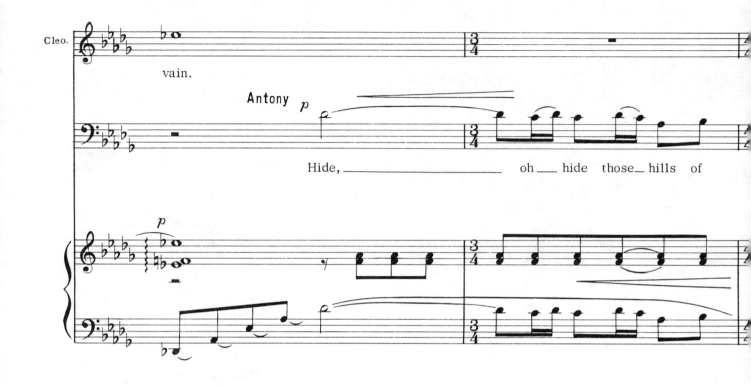

lips, _____ take those__ lips a -

bears, On whose tops the__pinks that grow are__those_____ that__ A -

way, _____ Take those lips a -

- pril__wears_____ But__ first _____ set my poor _____ heart__free,

Cleo:

way.

An

Bound in those i - vy chains by thee.

dim.

mp

(Reluctantly disentangling himself from Cleopatra's embrace, Antony gets up.)

espr.

marc.

marc.

pp

p

33 Antony

cresc.

E - ros!

Mine ar - mor,

leggerissimo

Cleopatra *(tenderly)*

Sleep a lit--tle. ____

E - ros!   No, ____

____ my chuck.   E - ros, ____ come, good

156

An.

fel-low, _____ put my i-ron on. If for-tune be not

sim.

(Eros comes into the tent,
bringing Antony's armor.

An.

ours to-day, _____ It is be-cause we brave her.

poco f

As he is about to fasten it on Antony, Cleopatra
pushes him away and takes his place.)

46074

158

46074

*A cut may be made from 36 to 39

stringendo e cresc. poco a poco

Attacca Scene 5

Scene 5
The Actium Battlefield

(The tent disappears, showing an open battlefield. It becomes day; the Egyptian army is seen marching off to battle.)

TENOR

BASS I

Trum-pet-ers, _____ with bra - zen

BASS II

Or - der for sea is giv - en. _____

Make min-gle with our

din _____ blast you the na - vy's ear;

They__ have put forth the__ ha - ven: _____

way!

way!

(As the flames of Cleopatra's burning fleet redden the sky, Egyptian soldiers are seen fleeing across the stage, throwing their weapons on the ground. Some are dragging wounded companions. A few of the dying are abandoned on the field.)

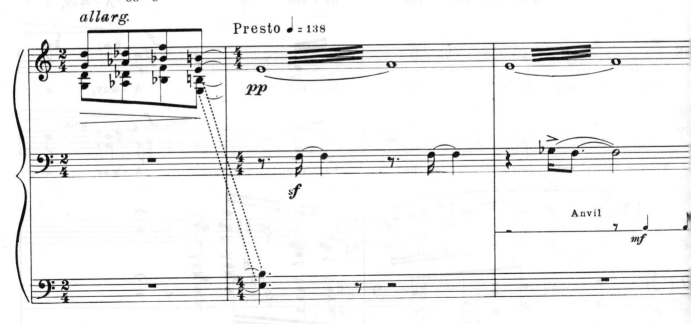

(Enobarbus enters in desperate anger, shortly followed by other Roman soldiers.)

Naught, naught, all ___ naught! I can be-hold no long-er.

The An-ton-i-ad, ___ the E-gyp-tian ad-mi-ral, With all their six-ty,

fly ___ and turn the rud-der:

To see it, mine eyes are blast-ed. ___

(Exeunt omnes.)

(On the desolate battlefield, littered with corpses, a few scavengers appear searching for loot.)

[49] **Allegro molto, quasi presto** ♩ = 152

182

(Enter Antony, Eros and a fe
wounded Soldiers. Antony su
veys the destruction of his
army.)

allarg.e morendo

46074

who __ With half the bulk of the world played __ as I pleased, ___

(Completely stunned, Eros sinks to his knees and bursts into loud sobs. Antony approaches

allarg. molto

Mak-ing and mar - ring for - tunes.

53 *him, and tenderly lays his hand on Eros' head.)*

Tempo I

Nay, __ weep not, gen-tle E - ros, There is left us

legato sempre

 our-selves   To   end _____ our - selves. _____

legato sempre

Fare - well,   O   friends. _____

allargando

(*Exeunt.*)

54 Molto allegro e marziale ♩=126

188

dim. sempre di più

Perc.

ppp

pp

attacca Scena

Scene 6

A Room in Cleopatra's Palace

Cleopatra is seated on her throne, surrounded by her court, while addressing Thidias, who is kneeling in front of her. Alexas, Charmian and Iras are standing near the throne.

I hear the doom of E-gypt.

Thidias *mf*
Give me grace to lay My

du-ty on your hand.

Your

Cae-sar's fa-ther oft, When he hath mused of tak-ing king-doms in,

espr.

Moon and stars! Whip him. So sau-cy with the hand of she here...

Whip him, fel-lows,__ Till like a boy you see him cringe his face_____

(free)

And whine a-loud for mer-cy!

Charmian *(suddenly struck with the idea)*

To the mon-u-ment. There lock your-self.

Iras

And send him word that you are dead.

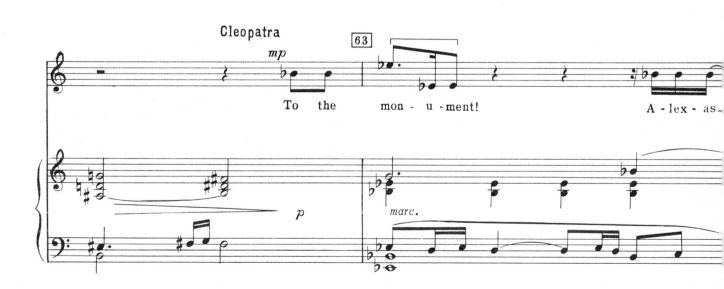

Cleopatra

To the mon - u -ment! A - lex - as-

198

46074

A Battlefield

Enobarbus is lying on the ground, supported by his shield.
In the background two soldiers watch him.

share in his booty, he walks off,
leaving Enobarbus alone on stage.)

moving ahead
cresc. poco a poco

broaden
ff

ver- -y reb-el____ to my will,   May hang no long-er on me.

69 Allegro molto ♩=100

Throw my heart____ A-gainst the flint and hard-ness of my fault,____

f martellato

Which, be--ing dried with grief,____ will break____ to pow-der,

(darkly)

And fin-ish all foul thoughts.____   This blows my heart.

f sub.

204

46074

attacca Scene 8

Scene 8

Inside Antony's tent. Night.

Antony is sitting on the couch, his head in his hands. Eros is standing near him.

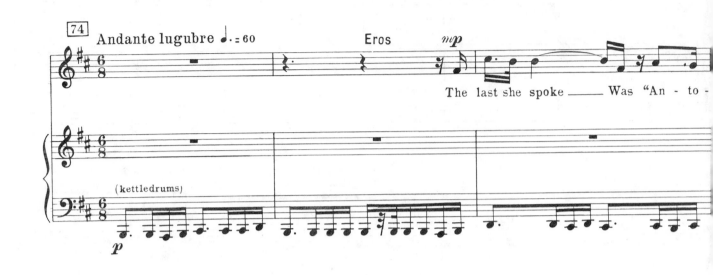

Eros: The last she spoke ___ Was "An - to -

Er. ny, most no - ble An - to - ny!" Dead. ___

Antony: Dead, then?

Un-arm, E-ros.

An. The long ___ day's task is done, ___ And we must sleep.

*) high-spirited

46074

Eros *(walking away from him in great anguish)*

Oh, sir, par - don me.__

An.

Do it, the time is come. Draw,__ do it at once.__

a tempo

p sonoro

mf espr.

Er.

Turn from me then that no - ble coun - te - nance __ Where-in the wor - ship __ of the whole world lies.

An.

mp

Er.

f

My sword is drawn.

(Antony turns from him and kneels down.)

An.

Then let it do at once The thing why thou hast

rall.

poco f

My— dear—mas-ter,— My cap-tain, and my em-per-or, let me say, Be-drawn it.

a tempo

fore I strike this blood-y stroke, fare-well. Fare thee well, great chief.— Shall I

(roughly)
'Tis said, man, and fare-well.—

strike now? Why, there then!— Thus do I es-cape— the sor-row—

Now.———

Er. Of An- to-ny's death._____

(He kills himself. 78 *Antony quickly turns, just in time*
to catch the falling body in his arm.)

An. Thrice-no - bler than my-self!

a tempo

An. Thou teach-est me,____ O val - iant E - ros. Come, then: thy mas-ter dies____

An. ____ thy schol-ar;____ to do thus____ I learnt of thee.____

allarg.

(*Antony falls o*
his sword.)

a tempo primo

(*free, anguished*)

79 (*Four or five of Antony's*
Guard enter.)

An. The guard, ho! O dis-patch me!

colla voce

f appass.

(Antony is carried out.)

star is fal-len and time is at his per-iod.

star is fal-len and time is at his per-iod.

A-las, a-las, and woe.

(Alexas, before leaving, approaches Eros' body and closes his eyes;
then he picks up Antony's fallen sword, and follows.)

End of Act II.

Act Three
Scene 1
The Monument
Cleopatra, with Charmian and Iras, stands on a high platform.
The entrance below is guarded by Egyptian soldiers.

(Enter Antony, carried by soldiers, some bearing torches.)

46074

Cleopatra

a tempo

mp

I dare not, dear;— Dear my lord,— par-don: I dare not, Lest I be tak-en. But come, come, An-

An.

lips.

a tempo

p espr.

Cleo.

allarg. **a tempo**

- to-ny! Help me, my wom-en, we must draw thee up: As-sist, good friends.

An.

(free) *f*

O quick, or I am gone.

allarg. **a tempo**

colla voce 3 *sfp colla voce*

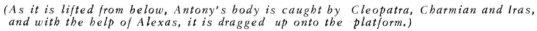

(As it is lifted from below, Antony's body is caught by Cleopatra, Charmian and Iras, and with the help of Alexas, it is dragged up onto the platform.)

9 Sostenuto e pesante ♪ = 60

mf

Here's sport in-deed! How heav-y weighs my lord! O come, ____ O come, ____ o ____ come. ____ My man of men! Help, ____ Char-mi-an, help, ____ I-ras, Help, friends be-low, ____ let's draw him hith-er.

that pow - er, _____ Thus, _____ thus would I wear them

E - - gypt; _____ my ser-pent of old Nile!

(Holding Antony's body in her arms, she kisses him.)
allarg. molto

out. _____

Charmian

Ah, heav - y sight! ____ Ah, heav - y sight! ____

Iras

Ah, heav - y sight! ____ Ah, heav - y sight! ____

allarg. molto

f espr.

The no - - - - blest:

and do___ not base - ly die.___

morendo poco a poco

A Ro - man, by a Ro - man val -

- iant-ly ——— van - quished.

Now my spir - it... is go - ing.

(Antony dies.)

I can no more! ———

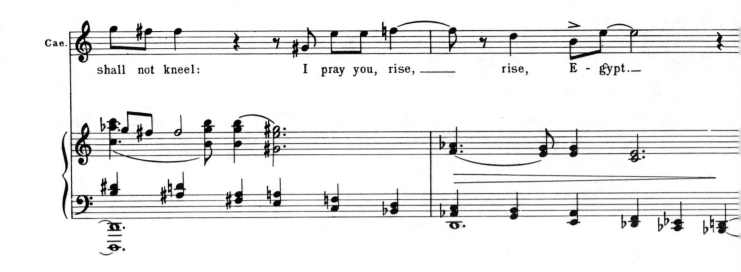

Cae.
shall not kneel: I pray you, rise, ___ rise, E - gypt. ___

a tempo, un poco più sostenuto

Cleopatra *poco allarg.*
Sir, the gods will have it thus. ___ My mas-ter and my

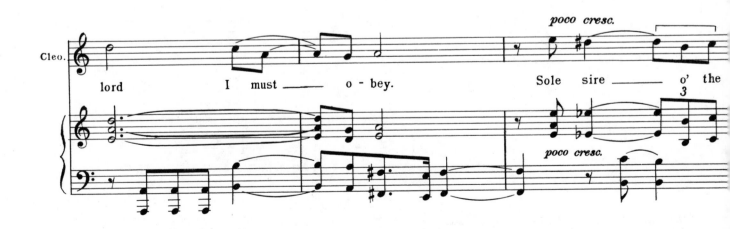

poco cresc.

Cleo.
lord I must ___ o - bey. Sole sire ___ o' the

world, I can-not pro - ject mine own cause so__ well

(hesitatingly)

To make it clear... **Caesar** *f (free)*

Cle - o - pa - tra, be cheered,——

colla voce

—— for we in-tend so to dis-pose you, As your-self shall give us coun-sel.——

(As Cleopatra is about to leave Caesar suddenly stops her.)

Caesar (kneels by Antony's body, lifts his sword, and holds it in front of him)

244

46074

broadening until the end

un-rec-on-cil-i-a-ble,___ our stars___ should di-vide Our

e-___ -qual-ness to this.___

(Caesar exits, while Alexas and Dolabella begin to lift Antony's body. Slow curtain.)

allargando e morendo

Prelude

31A

Andante maestoso, come una marcia ♩ = 56

Scene 2
Inside the Monument

(A throne stands in the middle of the room. Cleopatra is seen walking back and forth in great agitation, watched by frightened Charmian and Iras.)

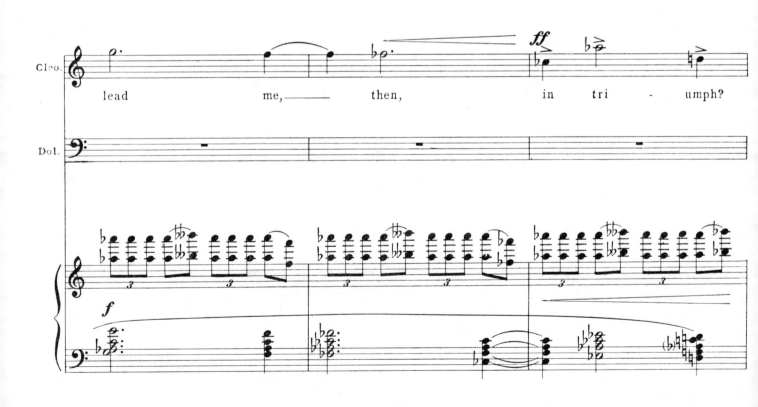

o' tune. Shall they hoist me up And show me to the shout-ing var - let - ry Of cen - sur - ing Rome?

(Charmian enters.)

Rath - er a ditch in E - gypt Be gen - tle grave un - to me!

Rath - er make My coun-try's high pyr - a - mi - des my gib - bet

258

46074

46074

260

46074

day how she died of the bit-ing of it, what pain she

felt. Tru-ly, ___ she makes a ver-y good re-port of the

Cleopatra

Ay, ay; fare-well.

worm. The worm's an odd worm. Give it noth-ing,—

266

(He sets the basket down and, having received a ring from Cleopatra, quickly exits. Immediately af.
Charmian and Iras enter with Cleopatra's robe and crown. Cleopatra steps down toward them.)

worm.

poco allargando

allargando molto

48 Andante maestoso ♩=50

Cleopatra

Give me my robe, put on my crown, ___ I have Im-mor-tal long-ings in me.

___ Now no more _____ The

46074

270

that I may say The gods them-selves do weep.

colla voce

53 **Cleopatra** *(grasping an asp in her hand)*
Agitato, faster than before ♩ = 80

Come, _____ thou mor-tal wretch.

mf (roughly)

With thy sharp teeth this knot in - trin - si-cate ___ Our life at once un-

(She applies another asp to her throat.)

Cleo. Nay,— I will take thee, too:

Cleo. What should I stay—

56

(Charmian reaches up for the basket and

Cleo. ...In this vile world?

♪ = 80, with supple motion

searches inside for an asp which she then applies to her own throat.)

sempre legato

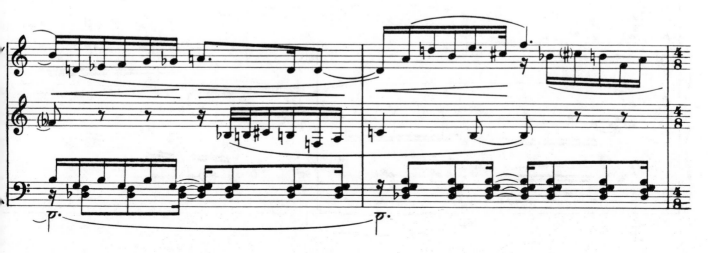

(Cleopatra dies. Charmian reaches toward her and dies. The basket falls from her grasp and rolls down the throne steps, spilling the figs.)

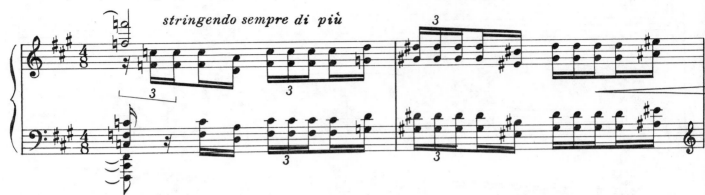

(During the following chorus the light on the stage will lower very slowly until, shortly before the curtain, only Cleopatra's face is to be seen.)

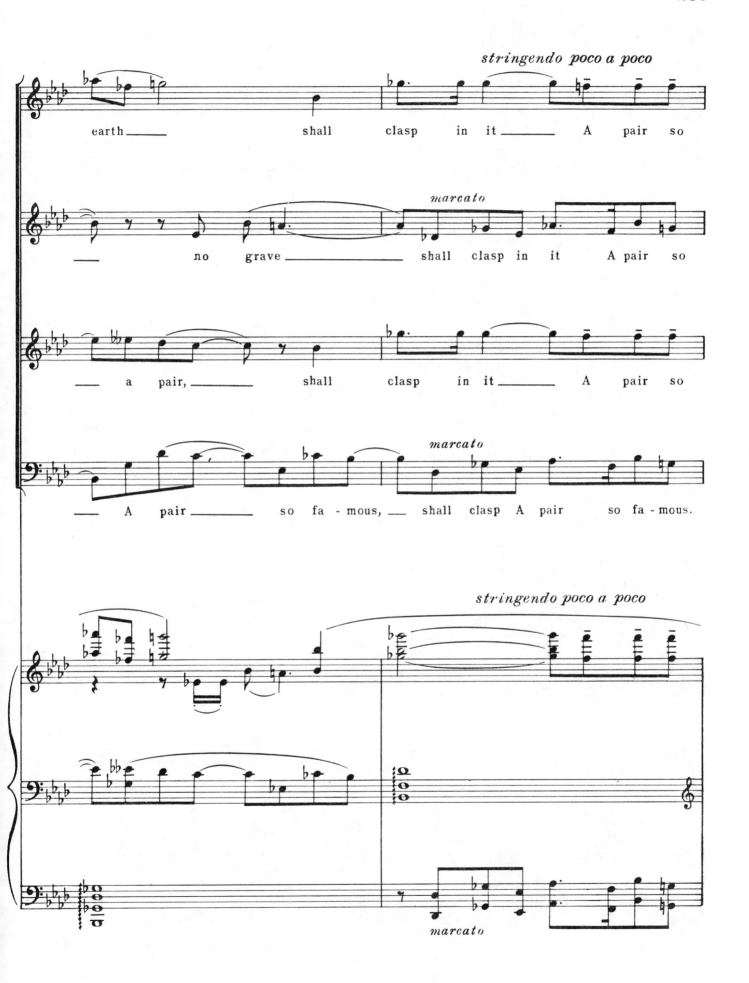

286

288

46074